INTERIOR
DESIGN
FOR
IDiots

**A SELF HELP GUIDE
TO INTERIOR DESIGN**

Cover Illustration by Design Dynamics, Glen Ellyn, IL.
Inside illustrations excerpted from
The Illustrator's Handbook, A & W Visual Library, New York, NY and
Decorative Frames and Borders, Dover Publications, New York, NY.

Published in Glendale Heights, IL by Great Quotations Publishing Co.
Printed in Hong Kong.

To my wife Diana,
without whom this little book would not have been possible;
and to my two sons,
Stephan and Christopher
who have taught me the true joy of living.
For my Dad.

Mark McCauley is a Professional Member of the American Society of Interior Designers (ASID). He is employed as a Senior Interior Designer by Marshall Field's, Chicago, IL.

I am a lucky man. As an interior designer I have been fortunate to meet many talented, wonderful people: My Clients.

My role has often been that of teacher, providing these clients with the *basic tools of interior design* while helping to instill in them a sense of *confidence* in their own taste.

Hopefully, this handbook will give you, whether you are moving to a new residence or redecorating your present one, some small bits of information to assist you along your way. Perhaps it will pique your interest in interior design. Perhaps it will lead you to more scholarly works on the subject. Perhaps it will make the perfect door-stop.

Whatever, interior design is a delightful process full of beauty and grace.

As I said, I am a lucky man.

Index

Part One

Realization
is the First Step
Towards Allure

Unfortunately, you are not a well person. You suffer from a chronic, progressive illness undiagnosed by the psychological profession. The disease is insidious. It envelopes the afflicted in a web of confusion, doubt and despair often leading to emotional and, quite possibly, financial ruin.

You are a Decoratively Challenged Individual, incapable of making even the slightest design decision regarding your home's interior without failing miserably.

It's been like this for years, hasn't it? It's okay, you can talk to me.

You've done everything. Bought all the right magazines, spent untold hours pouring over wallpaper books, squinted at fabrics until you are blind, searched endlessly for the perfect end table. But it's no use. You know it's true. Even though you try to hide it, try not to think about it. You know.

This is nothing to feel ashamed about. There are many like sufferers all over the country. People who dread the thought of visitors rolling on the floors of their homes, laughing and pointing. People who live in seeming time capsules exactly reproducing long dead fashions from 1967. People whose pets make better design decisions.

Pick the other
fabric, stupid!

Having come to terms with your affliction, let's examine its root causes.

Ever wondered why your neighbor's interior looks like it belongs on the cover of Architectural Digest while yours looks like a National Geographic photo essay on the Slums of Bangkok?

It's because your neighbor possesses a quality that you don't, namely: **Common Sense.**

Common sense tells you where to put things, what goes with what and to plan ahead. Common sense is **the** most important thought process involved in designing interiors.

We can now move on to the *most important aspect* of your home. Every home has one and no home would be a home without one. **YOU.**

The prime factor in decorating any environment is the person or persons living there and their individual needs and wants.

The most difficult aspect of interior design is answering the BIG QUESTION, the question that has plagued philosophers through the ages:

WHO ARE YOU?

What do you like? • What is your lifestyle? How do you really want to live?

In order to properly decorate your home it is necessary to come to terms with yourself and your inner life. You may now begin chanting your mantra.

What we're referring to here is the ***Development of Personal Style***, a much more important aspect of your home's decoration than any external object could possible have. A tastefully designed interior accurately reflects the inner world of the people living there.

The items in your home are given meaning and life through their association with you, not the other way around as is so often the case.

"We'll miss you son, but we couldn't afford 4 children <u>and</u> new drapes."

Pride of ownership is a wonderful feeling, yet it can also turn a home away from its intended purpose of shelter, comfort and emotional stability to one of self-serving one-upmanship.

We've established the roles common sense and your personality play in your home's decor. Our next task is to examine your likes and dislikes. Or:

The Definition Of Your Taste

Begin by studying the physical world around you. Research the topic by buying shelter magazines, visiting the library, examining your friend's homes, browsing furniture stores and, most importantly, *asking questions!*

Do not be afraid to ask questions! Remember, you don't do this for a living. How can you possibly know what's what in the design world if you don't ask questions?

Fire Away With Your Questions, It's The Only Way To Learn!

At some point in your research you will come across a photo or an object that will take your breath away. Your heart will skip a beat and, after being released from the Intensive Care Unit you will shout, *"Eureka! Sweet mystery of life, at last I've found you! Now what do I do?"*

First, calm down or you'll knock the IV out. Whatever you saw is probably way more than you can afford.

If it's a picture you saw in a magazine, tear it out. If it's a picture you found in a library book, don't tear it out; librarians tend to frown on that sort of thing.

Begin to collect photos of things that you respond to **immediately with emotion.** Don't overly concern yourself with the item's eventual end use.

The process you are involved in, by its very nature is an emotional one.

What you are looking for are objects or rooms that you respond to instinctively, with little or no thought.

By learning what these objects are, you learn about your various likes and dislikes. **You develop a Personal Style.**

As you discover your likes and dislikes, it's a good idea to also define who you are by the examining the circumstances surrounding your life.

The following discussion of the *Stages of Life* will help you determine your place in the world.

The Stages of Life

Age is a primary factor in ascertaining the taste levels of individuals. For this purpose we will divide the population of the United States into separate age groups.

0-5 years of age

If you fall between the ages of 0-5 you really should be concentrating on other aspects of your life, like walking, and leave the interior design to Mommy and Daddy. Your credit rating will be poor while your ability to do anything beyond staring trance-like at the television, drooling on your shirt and flinging food about wildly will be suspect.

5-10 years of age

Those of you in this age group are also likely to run into problems and ought to be doing your homework right now. If you have any serious design questions regarding Barbie's Dream House or the GI Joe Command Center it's best to ask Jason across the street.

Or his older sister Jennifer.

The Male

There is an interesting sub-group of 7-9 year olds within this category. We in the design trade refer to this as the *Me Tarzan, You Stain* period.

On a savage seek-and-destroy mission, 7-9 year old males will damage any items placed in their immediate vicinity.

Utilizing whatever means at their disposal they will devour upholstery, chew up carpeting and annihilate accessories. They treat furniture as a private, cushioned jungle gym provided for their own amusement.

They hurl themselves missile-like at couches from 10 feet away, perch on the top rails of chairs as if practicing for a future with the Flying Walendas and tilt and tumble their way toward adolescence.

A suggested parental response is removing all interior furnishings and replacing same with an automobile tire hung from a sturdy rope. A little straw on the floor wouldn't hurt, either.

10-15 years of age

Age 10-15 years represents the first awakening of interior consciousness. Human beings begin to develop the concept of *Their Own Space.*

This is typified by poorly scrawled signs reading **Keep Out** posted on bedroom doors and the ritualistic slugging of any little brothers who attempt to touch their stuff. Interior design for individuals in this stage usually consists of a single (preferably unmade) bed, strategic placement of clothing articles about the floor and dog-earred posters of societal icons, ie: various rock stars, athletes and movie idols thumb-tacked to walls in a haphazard fashion.

15-20 years of age

This group is preparing to leave the nest they've spent the better part of their lives soiling like so many seagulls.

These individuals are likely to be far too concerned with what to wear on Saturday night to concentrate on the niceties of interior design. Add to this a complete lack of funding and we have a style commonly referred to as:

"Mom can I have that 14 year old sofa in the basement? It really doesn't smell that bad" Look.

20-30 years of age

Undoubtedly the most important stage of human design development, this includes the defining *Young Married Style.*

This style is characterized by the creative use of cheap Scandinavian furniture to furnish a 3rd floor walk-up. This furniture is known as 'KD' for knocked-down or unassembled. It is also known as ***"Good luck trying to put this stuff together yourself as there are 7 million parts of which only 3 million are included and the assembly instructions are in Swedish" Look*** so popular with Laplanders.

This period also witnesses the early awakenings of true attempts at interior design by the *young wife.* Conversely, the *young husband* begins to retreat further and further from the design process as the *young wife* insists on shopping for wallpaper during the second quarter of the Super Bowl.

This is not met with enthusiasm on the part of the *young husband* and results in the development of the dreaded ...

Mother-Daughter Design Team

in which the mother of the *young wife* attempts to inflict her years of poor design decision making on the home of her daughter.

She literally devours her young in a design sense.

30-45 years of age

This is the age advertisers salivate over, ***The Age of Discretionary Income,*** during which one has secured one's place in society and can, with what little that's left over, actually afford a half-way decent chair to sit on or, with luck, a comfortable bed to sleep on.

Sleep fitfully, however, as hyena-like ***Home Furnishings Executives*** lurk unseen around the corners of your life.

They can sense the kill. Its scent sends them into a frenzy of activity. There is income left over, and they want it. They send clever subliminal messages such as

50 to 71 years of age

Also known as ***The Throw Back Years***, this period is defined by its individuals having made no meaningful design progress for the past 30 years, continuing to like what they like before the Beatles ruined everything.

A common symptom of the Throw Back Years is the atrophication of the Design Gland, located in the upper region of the hypothalamus. The root cause of this debilitating disorder is repeated viewing of antiquated fashion statements. Sound familiar?

72-116 years of age

Those in this stage of life should only concern themselves with the lobby of the retirement home their ungrateful children have relegated them to. Not to mention the fact that with the greying of America's baby boomers the whole country will be retired about 40 years from now, so what's the point?

We have now completed our journey through the Stages of Life. And you were wondering why you can't design your way out of a paper bag! Look at what you've been up against:

Destructive Children • Preying Mothers
Retreating Husbands • Uncaring Executives

A gamut of obstacles coming between you and the interior of your dreams.

All is not lost, however! By adhering to the principles set down in the following pages you too can produce a tastefully appointed interior.

All you need is:

- A little faith in yourself
- A little courage
- An unlimited supply of money

And your home can be transformed from this dump to, well, maybe a little nicer dump.

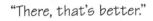

"There, that's better."

At this point in our discussions many of you
may still be wondering,
Am I truly a Decoratively Challenged Individual
or
maybe only legally blind?

The following:
In-Depth Personality Quiz To Determine Whether A Person Is Decoratively Challenged Or Simply Male
will help you to determine the extent
of your possible affliction.

Please use a #2 lead pencil only.

1. While sitting in your living room you have feelings of:

a) ❏ serenity

b) ❏ self-satisfaction

c) ❏ contentment

d) ❏ gut-wrenching nausea

2. Your family room is located:

a) ❏ at the back of your home

b) ❏ at the front of your home

c) ❏ off the kitchen

d) ❏ at your neighbor's home because you can't stand yours

3. Does your dining area resemble:

a) ❑ a quaint 18th Century English country dining room
b) ❑ a formal Victorian dining room
c) ❑ a contemporary California style eatery
d) ❑ the chuckwagon on Rawhide

4. Your carpeting reminds you of:

a) ❑ a lush, smooth lawn
b) ❑ soft grains of sand
c) ❑ the dark side of the moon

5. Your favorite chair style is:

a) ❏ Chippendale

b) ❏ Queen Anne

c) ❏ Regency

d) ❏ Folding

6. When choosing a personal style for yourself you:

a) ❏ research the topic

b) ❏ ask a friend

c) ❏ visit the library

d) ❏ call the Psychic Connection

7. When you go to sleep at night the last thing you see is:

a) ❑ a ceiling fan

b) ❑ a bed canopy

c) ❑ crown moulding

d) ❑ rafters

8. Your favorite color is:

a) ❑ red

b) ❑ blue

c) ❑ green

d) ❑ what exactly do you mean by the word color?

9. There are large holes in the walls of your home. These are:

a) ❏ doors

b) ❏ windows

c) ❏ areas behind paintings that resemble Swiss Cheese due to the fact that you can't hang a painting straight

10. Your window treatments consist of:

a) ❏ tastefully designed swags and jabots

b) ❏ horizontal blinds

c) ❏ windsor pleated draw drapes

d) ❏ the dog's old blanket

11. If you had enough money, you would:

a) ❏ buy a mansion

b) ❏ put an addition on your present home

c) ❏ redecorate your entire interior

d) ❏ get that mobile home you been a hankerin' for

12. The largest object in your home is:

a) ❏ the china cabinet

b) ❏ the armoire

c) ❏ the mortgage

13. Your previous decorating experience consists of:

a) ❏ helping decorate a friend's home

b) ❏ rehabbing a "builder's special"

c) ❏ putting the chairs away after the prison AA meeting

14. When was the last time you redecorated?

a) ❏ Within the past 6 months

b) ❏ 1985

c) ❏ 1975

d) ❏ Did what?

Tabulate Your Score

If you answered *c* or *d* to any of the above questions then unfortunately this book can't help you. In fact, nothing can.

If you *did not* answer *c* or *d* to any of the above questions, there is some hope, though not much.

If you didn't answer any of the questions you are a person of character who wouldn't stoop to attempting to understand their personality by answering a bunch of goofy questions. Way to go, you passed.

The Decoratively Challenged Individual may also suffer from other associated neuroses. Some of these ailments are listed below.

Fabriphobia

An unnatural fear of fabrics. Many Fabriphobics often give up hope altogether and join nudist colonies.

Sofa Anxiety

Stress caused by the inability to select upholstery fabric. This malady can often continue for years with the unwitting sufferer spending most of their time sitting on the floor.

Kitschophrenia

The display of large collections of objects which no one in their right mind could care less about such as empty beer can collections, world's fair programs or forks.

Recurring Roseanne Barr Disease

The decorating of a home based on the goodwill of others and a perusal of alleys prior to garbage day.

Accessoholism

Rampant over-accessorization of an interior to the point that the space resembles an airport gift shop.

Chronic Laura Ashleyism
The dripping femininity of exploding ruffles, frills, and fluff giving the home an unnerving sense that every ounce of masculinity has been wrenched from it.

Smithsonian Attic Syndrome
The collecting of items with little or no thought to their overall impact on the home's interior. your basic Garden Shed look.

"I'm sorry Bob, she's terminally Kitschophrenic."

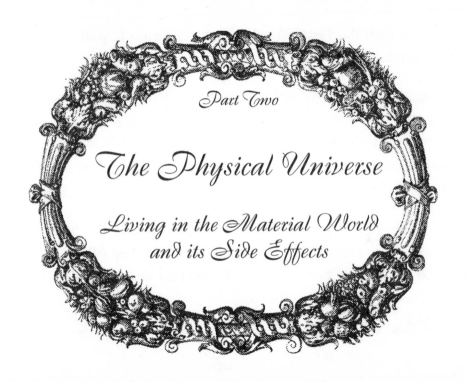

Part Two

The Physical Universe

Living in the Material World and its Side Effects

Although the Post-Woodstock Generation is loathe to admit it, we live in the *Material World*.

We all believe in our heart of hearts that the only proper way to live requires renouncing all of our worldly possessions, donning tie-dyed T-shirts and faded jeans, hanging out in psychedelic painted VW Micro Vans, grooving to Hendrix and saying things like, *Capitalism is such a drag.*

While this is quite an understandable desire, the bank usually won't stand for it. **It's the 90's, not the 60's** - there are children to raise, bosses to soothe and an unending stream of relatives to feed.

Baba Ram Das doesn't live here anymore.

The Material World demands our attention!

Maslow's Hierarchy of Needs (Physical, Shelter, Social) clearly defines the necessities of life. Notice how 'Tastefully Designed Interior' is not among these stated needs.

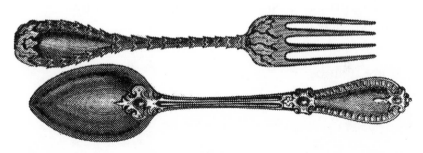

Our interiors, however, exert an inordinate amount of influence on our lives. A confused, chaotic mess of an interior indicates one of several things to the trained design professional:

1. You are working way too hard and need a long extended vacation.

2. You are a Decoratively Challenged Individual requiring proper design counseling and adequate chemical therapy.

3. You are a slob.

These patterns of behavior are created by a vicious cycle of events. You have no time to concentrate on the fundamental aspects of your home's interior, therefore, your interior deteriorates. This malady is known as: ***Decor-Addiction.***

Decor-Addiction afflicts more American homes than termites. It is responsible for over one half the reported cases of hysterical blindness in this country and results in numerous 'Taste Inflicted' lawsuits. Our court systems are clogged with such cases!

"Not another one."

With early enough intervention, however, this process is reversible. The affected parties often enjoy complete recovery through the use of group therapy. Many go on to lead meaningful, productive lives.

Decor-Addicts Anonymous (DecAnon) has attracted many followers with its hands-on approach and the adherence to a 12-Step Program to combat the disease.

Here, for the first time, released to the general public is the...

Decor-Addicts Anonymous 12-Step Recovery Program

Step 1 - Clean Your House

No interior design works unless this vital first step is taken. Cleaning the house does not mean a bi-monthly shifting of dirt from one side of the room to another. It means a studious attempt to remain semi-clean and neat. Your interior loves you, isn't it about time you loved it back?

Note: This step is highly susceptible to relapse, constant vigil is necessary!

Step 2 - Live Your Life

According to our little friend, H. D. Thoreau, most people lead lives of quiet desperation. We'll wander aimlessly about our homes hating the things around us yet never quite getting to the point of actually doing something about it.

Decide to stop being a slave to your interiors! Take action! Pick a period of time during which you have few outside emotional stresses and concentrate on planning the interior you've always wanted.

Remember To Plan Within Your Means.

"A well-decorated home is rarely the most expensively decorated home."

Step 3 - Provide an Adequate Budget

Before any other aspect of your interior is considered the budget for the project must be determined. You will, of course, exceed this budget, but you'll feel better when you do because at least you gave it a little thought.

Home furnishings always cost more than you think they are worth. Why? Because somebody, somewhere in these great United States had to build it, that's why. You can go to the hardware store, pick up some lumber, a few coils and polyurethane foam, but you can't build a sofa.

Assume 25% of the total price of the home as appropriate for decorating or whatever you can spare after the kid's braces are paid for.

Plan On Spending Approximately 10% Over Your Proposed Budget.

Step 4 - Stop Kidding Yourself

There are no Magic Bullets. There are no Quick & Easy, Do-It-Yourself, Home Handyman's methods of producing stunning interiors. Your interior design cannot be produced properly with a fastfood attitude. This may require a seachange in your personality. It may call for discipline, dedication and courage.

You May Have To Call 911.

Step 5 - Form Follows Function

Consider the functions which the room you are decorating or the objects you are purchasing must fulfill.

Your rooms must be divided by function as well. There are strong societal forces at work here. People expect to see things in their proper places. Your bedroom set would look pretty silly in the kitchen, wouldn't it?

Each room needs its own identity. Rooms without an established identity suffer from *Split Roominality.*

There is too much going on in the room, too many functions for the space. The room becomes confused, disjointed. Its sense of self weakens. Soon it begins to hang out with the wrong crowd, staying out later and later. You're confused, angry. A confrontation is inevitable.

To avoid this scenario, rooms must be assigned the proper function in the overall scheme of the home. Then, within this framework, items must be selected that enhance the rooms function, creating character and personality.

The Functionality Of Home Furnishings Eclipse Their Appearance.

Step 6 - Break It Down

Every space consists of design elements combined into a pleasing whole. Take on these elements one at a time. That's what designers do, they look at a room as components of an artistic design, not as a gigantic void that needs filling.

Build your room's look. Layer it, one element on top of another. Start by considering the background space, the walls, ceilings and floors. These are the largest areas of dimension in a room, they will set the tone for the space. Then work your way down from these larger spaces to even smaller considerations, furniture, window treatments and floor coverings. Finally, look to the smallest areas; accent pieces, plants and lighting.

At last you will reach the room's smallest component, dust, which you will spend the remainder of your natural life cleaning up.

Isn't This Fun?

Step 7 - Plan Your Work, Work Your Plan

Once you've decided on an intelligent, attractive design try not to stray too far from its principles. It will be difficult to do this at times as the temptation to screw up everything will be great.

Don't give in to whims and wishes. No matter how much you loved that piece you saw downtown yesterday, think before you plop it down in the middle of your living room.

Discretion Is The Better Part Of Value!

Step 8 - Life is a Process, Not an Event

Interiors develop over a period of time. They do not magically spring fully-formed from your forehead. They require patience, care and nurturing, not unlike a human life. Allow your rooms to grow, don't try to throw everything at them at once.

Home Wasn't Built In A Day.

Step 9 - The Future Is Now

You know what's coming down the pike: more children, immovable in-laws, etc. Don't ignore these factors when considering your interiors. Take a few minutes to visualize possible future uses for the different spaces in your home. Create rooms with multiple functions to take advantage of your available space. Remember *Step 5* here and don't assign too many tasks to one room or I can't be responsible for the outcome.

Plan Your Work, Work Your Plan.

Don't become locked into utilizing a space as the previous owners did. Look at your rooms with an unjaundiced eye. Treat them as Tabula Rasa that can perform any function. A spare bedroom can be a workout room. A dining room can be transformed into a family room.

Many people get it into their heads that they need to spend quality time in every room in the house on a regular basis. This isn't necessary, nor is it particularly pleasant. Give yourself some space for your tasks. Spend time in the rooms you are fondest of.

Be Happy, Not Cramped.

Step 10 - Seek Professional Help

If you are contemplating a large investment in your interior the smartest thing you can do is **hire a professional interior designer.** Note, I said professional, not your aunt.

Design professionals are design professionals for a reason. They possess more than a mere flair for decorating. Designers know the proper industry resources and contacts that you don't. They know who's who and what's what. They serve as your representative with subcontractors and manufacturers. Their experience is indispensable.

Don't Play Decorator - Hire One!

Step 11 - Keep Hope Alive

Don't quit! There will be many times during the design process that you'll feel like giving up. Stay the course!

Call a friend and talk about your feelings, your frustrations. Take a break from the project for a period of time, it's not going anywhere. Let what you've initially accomplished sink in for awhile and get a feel for which direction you'd like to go next. Allow your mind to refresh itself, returning to the project with new enthusiasm. This is not a race to see who finishes first.

Take It Easy.

Step 12 - Anything That Can Go Wrong Will

Interior design is not pretty. Errors and delays are going to occur. Prepare yourself for this inevitability. Being shocked, when that outrageously expensive dining table you've waited forever for, is delivered with a busted leg, is natural. Holding the delivery men hostage at gunpoint until it's repaired, isn't.

Everything will be made right in good time. It is in the best interests of the retailer and the manufacturer to keep you happy.

Stuff Happens.

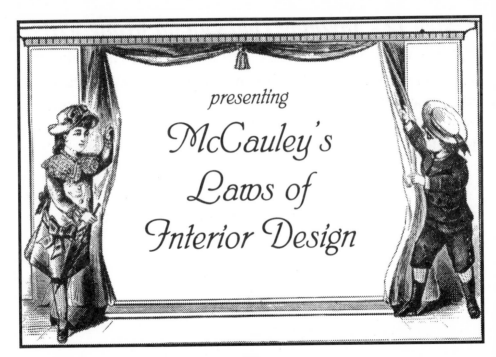

presenting

McCauley's

Laws of

Interior Design

McCauley's Laws of Interior Design

•If you love it, it's discontinued.

•The scratch is always in the most noticeable place.

•The sale ended yesterday.

• No one delivers to your town on Saturday.

•Service people don't, fabric protection won't, and delivery people can't.

•Your eyes are bigger than your wallet.

McCauley's Laws of Interior Design

•The last piece in stock will be broken.

•Absolutely nothing will turn the corners or fit up the stairs of your house.

•The cost of delivery is more than the object is worth.

•The cable outlet is always in the wrong place.

•A small, laser-like shaft of light will strike you right between the eyes at six o'clock every morning through a slit in your overly expensive black-out lined bedroom drapes.

McCauley's Laws of Interior Design

•Your mother won't get it, the kids won't like it, your husband won't pay for it and your best friend will tell you where you could have gotten it cheaper.

•You will never have enough closet space.

•The cat will cough up a hairball in the most obvious place on your carpeting.

•That expensive antique will turn out to be a clever reproduction which will unceremoniously be pointed out to you by a relative at your most important cocktail party.

McCauley's Laws of Interior Design

•The person with the greasiest hair will lay their head on the upholstery the most often.

•Someone, somewhere has bought the same piece for less.

•If you need a lock on a piece of furniture it won't come with one. If it has a lock, you will lose the key.

• Clearance items are clearance items for a reason.

• You will always notice the seams in your carpet.

McCauley's Laws of Interior Design

•The most beautiful sofa you have ever seen will be constructed in such a way that people will need a crane to get into or out of it.

•The lamp you've waited seven months for will be delivered without the finial.

•If you've just had white carpeting installed, the furniture delivery men will have tar on their shoes.

McCauley's Laws of Interior Design

•Everyone you've ever met is an interior design expert.

•You didn't figure for tax.

•The color you pick, which has been in fashion for years now, will suddenly and without warning be hideously out of fashion minutes after you take delivery.

•You will find out too late that the electrician is uninsured.

• Pets don't care.

McCauley's Laws of Interior Design

• One child will always want to sleep on the bunk that the other child insists on sleeping on.

• Human beings cannot choose paint colors from 2" color swatches.

• Young boys have terrible aim.

•Your old sheets will not fit the new mattress.

• You should have spent the money on a trip.

The Five Senses

**Congratulations,
you are the proud owner
of five senses.**

These sensory apparati do not automatically shut down upon entering your home. They are, in fact, extremely important to the creation of a well designed interior.

Vision

Most people look but do not see. Seeing a room is experiencing it visually. Looking at a room is blowing it off.

How does one see a room? By visually dismantling the space into its component parts, concentrating on each component separately then integrating the entire view into a whole.

Simple, huh?

Hearing

The sense of hearing has destroyed more interiors than all of the other senses combined. By listening to the wrong person you risk the entire project.

Certain people are not going to get your interior design, no matter what you do. They will raise their eyebrows, sniff and shrug their shoulders. And then do you know what they will do? They will go home, that's what they'll do.

"I can't wait to return home to my perfectly decorated interior. Your place is a real dive."

Taste

Taste is an outgrowth of knowledge. The more you experience life, the higher your level of taste. No one is born with an instinctive sense of style, not even Ralph (Lifshitz) Lauren, late of the Bronx, not exactly a hot-bed of haute couture. Education, travel and self-awareness all help elevate your taste level.

Large amounts of cash alone does not equate to good taste.
Ask Madonna.

Touch

The sense of touch is a highly underrated facet of interior design. The soft hand of fabric, the cool smoothness of metal or the warmth of beautiful wood all enhance a home's interior.

A piece can look terrific but upon closer inspection with the sense of touch it can lose its attractiveness.

Quoth the Bard, Peter Townshend:
> *"See me, feel me, touch me."*

Smell

Kill your rooms. Ruin them beyond repair. Disgust visitors, family members and pets. All that's required to accomplish this is to inflict extreme odors on your interiors.

And not just bad odors, either. Overuse of pot-pourri has sent many a guest reeling. Lemon freshness has been known to asphyxiate laboratory rats.

Be wary of this trap, it is easy to fall into. Let your nose be your guide as you lightly provide ambience with delicate scents.

The Five Senses form the basis of our information gathering processes. Combined, they create your sixth sense or **Sense of Style**.

Your **Sense of Style** tells you what goes with what and what appeals to you. This is extremely important in designing your interior as, without it, your home loses its individuality and becomes a mere collection of objects. Kind of like living in the garage.

The *Five Senses* send signals to our brains regarding the immediate environment.

This immediate environment is formed by a variety of elements. The combination of these elements creates our individual *Lifestyles*. Answering the questions in this *Lifestyle Profile* will help you to determine the specific requirements of your life.

1. Who lives in your home?
  a. Number of adults ___
  b. Ages ___
  c. Approximate Neck Sizes ___

2. Number of children
  a. Ages___
  b. Decibel level ___

3. Number of visiting relatives a 6.2 earthquake on the Richter Scale couldn't dislodge ___

4. Do you own any pets? Yes___ No___

5. Do your pets own you? Yes ___ No ___

6. What changes do you anticipate?
   a. Your children will grow up, leave the house and never call except to borrow money.
   b. Your children will grow up and never leave the house.

7. Where do you live?
   a. The crowded, noisy polluted, dangerous city
   b. The crowded noisy polluted, dangerous suburbs
   c. Some filthy backwater

8. Why do you live there?
   a. This is the town I was born and raised in
   b. My employer transferred me here
   c. The halfway house was full

9. How's the weather there?
   a. Too damn hot
   b. Too damn cold
   c. Both

10. Do you have a good view?

    a. Yes

    b. No, my cell bars get in the way

11. How will you finance these purchases?

    a. Cash

    b. Credit

    c. Wait until the convenience store clears out of customers, leaving fewer eyewitnesses.

12. What is your

    a. Age ___

    b. Height ___

    c. Weight ___

    d. No, your real weight ___

13. You are
   a. left-handed
   b. right-handed
   c. under-handed

14. Your personality is
   a. out-going
   b. introspective
   c. abnormal

15. What season are you?
   a. Winter
   b. Summer
   c. Spring
   d. Oregano

Part Three

The Hysterical Society

*A brief guide to perhaps
the world's most boring topic-
Period Design & Furnishings*

Our forebearers began the long, slow trudge toward civilization in places like Babylon, Assyria and Egypt.

Ancient Babylonian and Assyrian interior design is of little interest to anyone but Indiana Jones. Egypt, now that's another matter. These guys had style. Not only did they have a hot look going but they had the good sense to preserve it for us.

Those Ancient Babylonians and Assyrians left us a couple of crummy mounds and writing, big deal.

The Egyptians, on the other hand, had this wacky belief that you needed everything from this world to help you get by in the next. So, they buried all this great stuff with their dead pharaohs and we came around several millennia later, dug it up and stuck it in museums.

Since we've gone to all the trouble of knocking the dirt off these items, historians generally pick Egypt as the jumping off point for discussing period design. We don't want to rock the historical boat here, so we'll start with Egypt.

WALK LIKE AN EGYPTIAN

The world owes an enormous debt to the culture of Ancient Egypt. The art forms and architectural styles invented there are influential to this day. Independent of foreign influence, Egypt's isolation led to the repetition of basic styles for thousands of years. This was largely due to the fact that Egypt is so darn hot that no one ever visited, much less stayed the whole summer.

So as not to get too bogged down in the details of Egyptian decorative fashion, all you really need to know is:

1. The Egyptians pretty much invented furniture.

2. They substituted stone for wood as a building material cause there ain't no trees in the desert.

3. They had no perspective on things.

4. They were short.

Somewhere along the line the ability to draw with perspective was misplaced by the Egyptians. Their artwork is typified by two dimensional characters, the human form shown in profile. And usually just their good sides, too.

Religious symbols and hieroglyphics adorned their walls. These religious symbols depicted the various Egyptian deities such as the Sun god Ra and the other gods Re, So, Fa, La, Ti and Doe a deer, a female deer god.

These folks were also nuts for building huge geometrically shaped objects. This was probably in reaction to their own short stature, a way of compensating for being the butt of all those Assyrian short jokes.
They ran up astronomical bills in the process.

That room addition of yours looks pretty cheap in comparison to the Great Sphinx doesn't it?

IT'S ALL GREEK

IT'S ALL GREEK TO ME

We're talking influential here. The Ancient Greeks managed to invent government, rational western philosophy and the gyros sandwich while for fun on weekends they built the Parthenon.

They built the Parthenon without mathematics, too. Yep, just eye-balled the thing and slapped it up. Your high school teachers had it all wrong, none of that math nonsense is necessary. Ask any Ancient Greek.

The Ancient Greeks were also big into sculpting all kinds of funky urns and columns.

They also invented the klismos chair and the turned leg.

The klismos chair sits precariously on sabre legs. It has a distinct back rail that curves around the body effectively cutting off the circulation of blood to the brain.

Turned legs look like a stack of plates and are produced by turning a block of wood on a spit-like device over a blade until it's well done. Or medium rare.

ROMAN HOLIDAY
(See Greek)

Actually what the Ancient Romans did was refine Greek artistic forms. Refining is a process whereby one culture steals another's decorative style, then wrecks it.

In 79 A.D. Mt. Vesuvius erupted burying Pompeii and Herculaneum. This preserved them until the 18th Century. By 1753 most of these towns had been excavated, although a good portion is still underground as the people living there refuse to give up their homes for the sake of science. Ingrates.

A group of Ancient Romans carrying off
Greek decorative accessories.

Gothic Horror Stories

Now here's an age worth spending a little time with. This is the age of cathedral and castle, knights and ladies of chivalry, Crusades and the ever popular Bubonic Plague. If the wolves in the streets didn't get you, disease would and, if all else failed, your friends burned you at the stake as a witch.

This led to people doing an awful lot of praying. Enter Stage Left: The Cathedral.

Simultaneously, the rich and famous were busy finding new ways to fling objects at one another. This led to the development of the castle.

The signature room of the Medieval Castle was the Great Room which was, frankly, pretty great. There was a nice big fire going in the middle of the room and, if you could stand all the smoke, life was good.

The numero uno art form in the Gothic world was tapestry weaving. Suits of armor were a close second. Both were primarily meant to keep one alive. Tapestries were hung on walls to keep out drafts and armor was hung on bodies to keep out arrows.

Renaissance Redux

The rebirth of classical Grecian and Roman art forms is the dominant feature of the Renaissance style. After the seemingly endless drag of the Gothic, the Italians began looking around at their artistic and architectural progress and decided it wasn't really progress after all.

They were surrounded by all these great Roman ruins. Everywhere they looked they saw reminders of past glory. Funny thing was, this broken down stuff looked better than what they were currently producing. The Italians got the brilliant idea of re-birthing these artistic forms and another of the world's great artistic heists was on.

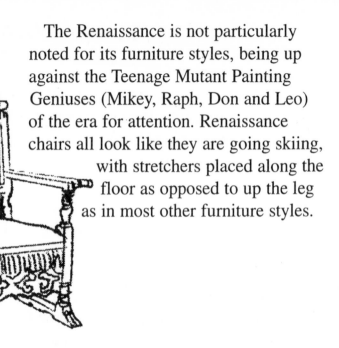

The Renaissance is not particularly noted for its furniture styles, being up against the Teenage Mutant Painting Geniuses (Mikey, Raph, Don and Leo) of the era for attention. Renaissance chairs all look like they are going skiing, with stretchers placed along the floor as opposed to up the leg as in most other furniture styles.

The French Connection

The French couldn't leave anything alone. French style is a veritable Fun House of curves on curly cues on squiggles without a straight line in sight.

The words used to describe French decorative forms make you sound like an idiot when you mispronounce them and are corrected by some well-meaning soul who wants to show you up because they took French 101.

The following Guide to *French Design Term Pronunciation* will help you pronounce these words without putting your tongue in traction.

Armoire (Are•em•whar):
A ponderously large, supposedly portable, closet. One would need a team of Clydesdales to move it. The French developed this Godzilla of a furniture piece because they forgot to put closets in their homes.

Bergere (Bear•jer):
Literally translated to English as *Chair for those who like upholstered arms on their chairs.*

Bombe (Bomb•bay): Not a town in India but a serpentine or curved bow front to furniture. Only a sick mind would torture wood this way.

Chaise Lounge (Chays Lounge): A piece of upholstery in which no one can decide whether to sit or lie.

Faux-Tois (Fo•toy): A French chair form designed by the same guys who forgot the closets only this time they forgot to upholster the sides of the chair.

Jacques Cousteau (Jak Coo•Stow): What French glossary would be complete without a mention of our buddy Jak?

Ormolu Mounts: Hey! Here's one that's pronounced exactly how it's written! Ormolu mounts are garish looking clumps of metal resembling bowling trophies plastered all over French furniture for no apparent reason.

Versailles (Ver•sigh): The palace of Louis XV, the Sun King. The ultimate case of way too few having way too much.

Singerie (Song•jer•i): Monkeys. Go figure.

Pox Britannica

The zenith of man's attempts to bend wood are represented in the English 18th Century furniture forms. Their grace and proportion leave everything in the dust.

The Fab Four: Chippendale, Adams, Sheraton and Hepplewhite, worked in distinctive styles that, along with the Queen Anne style, are easily identified.

Thomas Chippendale didn't really invent the Chippendale style of chair. What he did was pen a little book in 1754 titled ***The Gentlemen and Cabinet Maker's Director*** in which he catalogued the furniture styles prevalent at the time.

Chippendale chairs have a pierced back splat and yoke top rail which looks like the yoke you would put on the family ox. They incorporate straight or cabriole leg and the ball and claw foot.

Robert Adams helped out greatly by inventing the sideboard. His pieces have straight tapered legs and incorporate ancient motifs as Pompeian style.

George Hepplewhite designed chairs with straight legs and compass curve backs. These backs include the round, oval, camel, heart shaped and shield. There are no original Hepplewhite chairs still in existence as they've all been busted into kindling by overweight relatives just after asking, *"Do you think this chair will hold me?"*

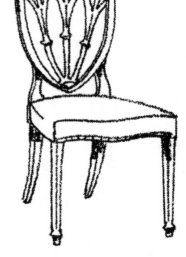

Tom Sheraton designed chairs similar to Georgie's with the notable exception that his chair backs are rectangular in shape.

America, The House Beautiful

Re-read this chapter. We ain't done nothing that no one else didn't come up with first unless you count bean bag chairs, drive-thrus, and the most serene environment ever devised, the Jiffy Lube waiting room.

The prime motivator here is that the French lost the French and Indian War to the English, otherwise we'd all be sitting on bergeres and reclining on chaise lounges.

"But Hillary, you know I hate mauve!"

The Minor Styles

These, of course, aren't minor styles to the people who have spent generations developing them, but they are to us because we're so high falutin' here in America having won the big one, WWII.

Oriental

Oriental rooms have an air of serenity missing in the west. Maybe that's because the west has appropriated every cool looking Oriental artistic device since Perry found Japan. The Far East has given us the Japanese Throne Chair, Altar Table, the Tonsu Chest and Nintendo among countless other influences.

Flemish

The Dutch Masters made more than cigars. Their contributions to the history of furniture include the bulbous leg, paint brush foot and Flemish scroll.

German

The Germans gave the world Beidermeier. This is the perfect style to impress your friends with. Just say, *Oh, that's Beidermeier* and they'll treat you with awe and respect because it sounds like you really know what you are talking about.

African
A brightly colored, naturalistic style better left in the bush.

Native American
Archeaologists that can't get a grant to travel to Egypt love this stuff. *See African for best use.*

Russian
Really bad copies of European styles as the Russians were always trying to play catch-upski after 400 years of Mongol rule.

Thus ends our brief journey through the history of Period Design and Furnishings.

Do you want to know a secret? **You are living in the most fabulous period in the History of Home Fashion!** That's right, America in the 1990's is an **interior design utopia!**

Home furnishings are made better, safer and more affordable than ever before.

Any style, a rainbow of colors, lighting that delights and incomparablely comfortable upholstery are all available to you.

Part Four
The Power of Positive Pinking

*Color
Theory
for
Real
People*

You, being a fine, upstanding member of the human race, have color vision. Your eyes perceive color.

This is one of life's little bonuses for us Homo Sapiens. Your dog doesn't have color vision, his life is one long 50's television show. The human eye, on the other hand, can distinguish between approximately ten million different colors. That means there are approximately 10 million different mistakes you can make. There, feel better?

Fortunately science has eliminated 9,999,997 of these colors leaving us with *three primary colors:* red, blue and yellow.

There are also a bunch of secondary, tertiary, quaternary, quintenery and ad infinitumary colors just to confuse you.

Color experts call these **hues**. Blue is a hue. When you say *I hate the color blue*, what you mean is that you hate the blue hue. Boo hoo.

Color also has **value** or the amount of light a color reflects. A color can have a light value or a dark value or it can be of no value whatsoever.

The third and last quality of color is **intensity**. This is the relative strength or purity of a color.

Got all that? Well, frankly, it's all hues to me.

The main reason that you don't know how to use color is because this is how it's always been explained to you. Some psycho mumbo jumbo about hues, values and intensities. No one ever tells you how to apply these concepts to your home.

Follow the simple formulas on the next pages and you'll be a color expert in no time.

Decorate Your Rooms In Colors You Look Good In.

Dressing a room is the same as dressing yourself, only larger...sometimes.

The same components go into a room's dressing process as go into your dressing process. Check out what is in your closet. Study the colors that you look good in, colors that you obviously like, since you bought them.

Divide Your Room's Colors
Into Components of 60-30-10

Use this simple formula to divide the colors in your room and you will knock 'em dead every time:

60% of a dominant color
30% of a secondary color
10% of an accent color

This, once again, goes back to how you dress. Say you are wearing a suit: 60% is the jacket and pants/skirt, 30% is the shirt or blouse, 10% is the neck tie or jewelry.

Take A Cue From Mother Nature

An interior environment is our attempt to recreate the outside environment. It is a small, all too human effort at making our own earths, our own worlds.

Knowing this, use the clues ol' Mom has provided. Decorate your rooms from relatively dark to light as you move vertically in the space, i.e.; a darker value for the floor, medium for the walls and lighter for the ceiling (ground, trees and sky. Get it?).

Tradition, Tradition

Do what everyone else does, steal ideas. Other people have already suffered through this process and, through trial and error, developed pleasing color schemes that you can claim as your own.

Local Color

All areas of the country are associated with particular color-ways. The East, The Midwest, South and West all have very distinct looks. Living in a particular geographic region provides a basic jumping off point for color selection.

Color Scheming 101

The type of color scheme you choose will impact how the space feels. There are three basic color schemes you can select:

Complementary - A very active color combination consisting of colors opposite each other on the color wheel, such as: Red-Green (Merry Christmas) or Yellow-Violet (Happy Easter).

Analogous - Colors that appear right next to each other on the color wheel. They are families of color. Sometimes dysfunctional families, but families, nonetheless.

Monochromatic - Varying shades of the same color. These rooms can be very effective or can induce comas.

Function is the key as to which color scheme to choose. If the space is active use complementary colors. If it is passive utilize an analogous color scheme. If it's complete boredom you want, monochromatic is your best bet.

Choose The Largest Pattern First

That's right. When it comes to color forget those walls and floors for starters. Head right out to the furniture store or fabric showroom and start flipping through fabrics.

The odds are that you will be locked into certain colors depending on how someone you'll never meet in New York or Paris likes them. You are at the mercy of these people. Picking the largest pattern first, instead of painting the walls and finding out you'll have to repaint because none of the colors match, is much easier. Cheaper, too.

Choosing The Right Colors Is As Easy As One, Two, Three.

1. Decide on a color scheme.
2. Vary the shades in the space from dark to light.
3. Pick the largest pattern first.

Add to this a little 60-30-10 and you're set for life - or at least through next month when the fashion changes.

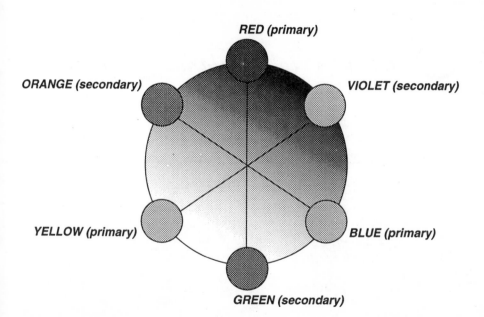

Part Five

Space - The Final Frontier

Your home presents you with many dilemmas. You can't squeeze enough people into the family room without injuring somebody. Every door swings the wrong way. Your hallways were built for ants.

You didn't notice these things when you bought the place did you? No, you were too busy checking out the schools, measuring the lot size, reading the mortgage to notice that you were about to purchase a home with nowhere to sit.

Let's combat the *Spacial Olympics* your home throws at you. We'll begin by breaking it down room by room.

Living Room
Remember this place? It's filled with furniture made for lookin' at rather than sittin' on. Many homes aren't complete without velvet ropes to preserve the look and to keep the riff raff *(family)* out.

Family Room
The heart of the home. Where everyone hangs out, puts their feet on the cocktail table and gets crumbs all over the place.

Dining Room
The place with so many special memories: Thanksgiving, Hannukah, Christmas, Food. The major problem presented by this space is how to use it the other 360 odd days of the year that aren't holidays.

Kitchen
That cheery, uplifting place people spend hours slaving and sweating in.

Master Bedroom
The largest bedroom in the house reserved for the people who pay the largest thing in the house, the mortgage.

Study
The only room in the house designated for use by the Pater Familias, Ol' Dad. Of course, Ol' Dad never gets to use the study for studying being out of town on business most of the time obtaining money to pay for the study. Dad's study is usually a Holiday Inn room in Tucson.

Spare Bedrooms
A convenient place to store children until they ripen.

Bath
Bathrooms improve the quality of life dramatically while providing vacation homes for the genius who invented tiny, scrubbing bubbles.

Basement
Cold, dank, dreary place often transformed into a cold, dank, dreary family room.

Garage
Your car's house.

Furniture Estrangement

Identifying these rooms is only half the battle. The real question is: How do you arrange the items in these rooms properly?

The arrangement of objects in a room has a dramatic psychological effect on the people using it on a daily basis and on visitors whom we're all trying to impress. One can arrange furniture in a welcoming fashion or one can say, "Take a hike, you unwanted guest, you."

Measure For Measure

The first step in arranging a space is **determining its size**.

We do this with a handy little device called a tape measure. If you're too lazy to measure an entire room, here's a quick way to gauge a room's dimensions. *Measure your foot.* Once you've measured your foot walk heel to toe across the room. You'll feel pretty silly doing this, but at least you'll get the job done.

The Write Stuff

You can't possibly remember all these sizes without writing them down, either.

Get a scrap of paper and draw a box on it.

Note the room's dimension next to the corresponding walls on the paper. You now have a bird's eye view of the room from above.

Place windows and doors in their approximate places on the page.

Be sure to measure the size of entryways and hallways. Furniture does not instantly materialize in a room once you buy it. It must be transported there. The worst experience in decorating is falling in love with a piece, then sitting by dejectedly as the delivery men tell you the west side of your house has to be removed before they can squeeze the piece in.

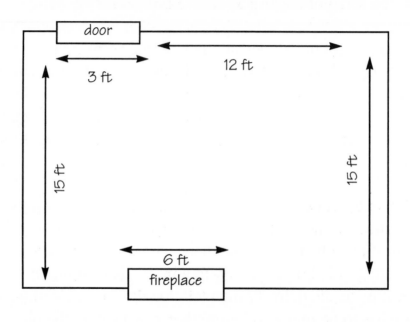

Scaling, Scaling Over the Bounding Main

The size of pieces relative to each other and the room's size is their **scale**.

A piece can be in scale, out of scale or off the scale. It can be too large for an area, too small for an area or just right. Get the picture, Goldilocks?

Pump Up The Volume

Volume is like people, There are short people, tall people, fat people, skinny people.

Objects are like people, they have the same physical characteristics as we do, except they can't join Weight Watchers.

Balancing Acts

The relationship of pieces to each other to form a pleasing whole is **balance**.

There is asymmetrical balance and symmetrical balance. Asymmetrical balance is off a little. Symmetrical balance is like your body, there are two of everything. Which leads to proportion.

Keeping Things In Proportion

In life, you keep things in proportion by giving them the right amount of attention and respect. Not too much, not too little.

In art, you keep things in **proportion** by choosing similarly **scaled** objects which seen together provide **balance** although they have different **volumes**. Piece of cake, right?

Paint Your Wagon

Painter's use techniques to create paintings that you can use in decorating a room.

Imagine the room as a blank canvas. Flat. No depth.

The first trick painter's use is **triangulation**. Build the room up from the sides of the canvas, lower in the corners to the apex of the triangle in the room's center. For example, put end tables on each corner, a sofa in the middle and a painting above the sofa. See the triangle? The top of the triangle is at the top of the artwork above the sofa. You now have a **background**.

Depth of a Salesman

We next add **depth** to the room by providing a foreground, a midground and a vanishing point.

Place an object closer to the viewer, say a chair. Now place an object between the chair and the sofa, a cocktail table. You now have a **foreground** and a **midground**.

A **vanishing point** is the place where your eye can go no further. Let's say your painting is of a landscape. The vanishing point would be in the painting. Your vanishing point could also be the view out your windows.

Gestalt, Baby

All arrangements of objects have a totality, a form, a *Gestalt*. Try to place like forms with like forms. For instance, a sofa with a loveseat has a square form when viewed from above. Use a square cocktail table with this form.

A sofa with a chair on each side, however is rectangular in form. Use a rectangular cocktail table with this.

Doing The Splits

Your rooms are probably large rectangles. This is difficult for our brains to justify psychologically.

Divide this large rectangle into squares, **split it down the middle**.

You accomplish this by dividing the space into **zones of function**. One square is for the upholstery group or the function of conversation. The other square is reserved for the dining area. Dividing your rooms into zones of function brings difficult spaces to their knees.

Those Vocal Focal Points

There is something in every room crying out for immediate attention, other than your children.

These are called a room's **focal points**. They are large elements such as doors, windows, fireplaces, china cabinets and your brother-in-law who was only staying for a few weeks until he got his life straightened out but is now a permanent fixture.

Try not to slosh all the focal points onto one side of the room. Balance your room's focal points, place them opposite from one another - armoire across from the windows, the china cabinet opposite the door...

There is another extremely important focal point in your home. ***The TV.***

This is the only focal point that anyone ever pays attention to for longer than 30 seconds. In fact, most people pay more attention to this than their spouses. Remember to consider the TV as one of the room's focal points and balance it with the others.

One other quick TV Guide - Optimum viewing for a normal sized television is approximately 8 feet. Don't place seating so far from the television that you need binoculars to see it.

Traffic Flaws

Now that you have selected the furniture, how do you get at it?

By building a city. The town you live in has houses. These houses are separated by streets. Arrange your rooms the same way. Provide major thoroughfares, side streets and alleys. You can even throw in a park or two for Sunday afternoons.

The **major traffic flow** of the room should be about three feet wide. **Minor traffic flows** around furniture should be approximately two feet wide. Provide space between the pieces of furniture theses are your alleys, to allow you to access them.

Buy a plant or two and you've got a park. A little bit of nature stuck in a corner of the room lessens the corner's severity. Interior designers hate corners, so should you.

You have now conquered your home's physical arrangement. Your home is more organized and visually appealing. You're actually starting to like it. Call the realtor and tell them to cancel the Open House, you're staying!

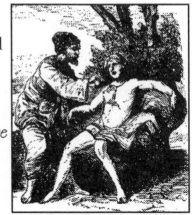

"Take it easy- we think you're a heck of a salesperson, but we just don't want to list our house!"

Part Six

Background Check

You live in a cube. Or, more correctly, a bunch of cubes stuck together.

These cubes are composed of several elements. They are: floors, ceilings, and walls. Amazingly enough, these cubes can be decorated. They needn't stay beige and white for eternity.

Let's look at these elements one at a time.

Floors

This is the area of your home near your feet. It can be created in a variety of different manners.

Carpeting - Probably the most prevalent means of decorating today, wall-to-wall carpeting is affordable, adds warmth to a room and is great for hiding pine needles for six months.

Hardwood Floors - The beauty of wood flooring enhances a room, however, it is colder and louder than wall-to-wall carpeting. Furniture tends to ice skate across its surface unless it's nailed down.

Oriental Rugs - Oriental rugs come in a plethora of different styles and sizes. Of course, the perfect style will not come in the size you require and vice versa but at least you've got choices.

Vinyl Flooring - Versatile, inexpensive and long wearing. Primarily used in high traffic areas, like grade school cafeterias.

Masonry - Stone, marble and brick is extremely durable, while giving your home that beautiful parking lot feel.

Dirt - Undoubtedly the most durable of flooring materials, dirt is, unfortunately, difficult to clean.

Walls

Walls are the largest vertical area of your home. You will recognize them immediately by their off-white color.

Paint - The easiest and least expensive wall treatment, paint is available in a wide variety of colors, and can give warmth and variety to a home. It also gives warmth and variety to the places where you spill it.

Wallpaper - A beautiful alternative to paint, wallpaper is readily available and comes in a gazillion different patterns and colors. You can easily estimate the amount of wallpaper needed for a room by measuring the height and width of the walls then dividing by how much money you have.

Wood Paneling - Adds warmth and that special VFW Hall ambiance to your home.

Masonry - Stone and brick are somewhat colder than the treatments mentioned above but at least you'll know that big bad wolf can't huff and puff and blow your house in.

Ceilings

Your ceiling provides many benefits other than keeping rain out. Ceilings can add formality or informality to a room depending on their height, coloration and decoration.

Treat your ceilings as a fifth wall in the home, don't ignore them; they're very sensitive and are easily offended.

Part Seven

Window

Mistreatments

There are a myriad of different window styles. All windows, however, fall into one of the three following categories:

1. Moveable - can be opened.
2. Fixed - cannot be opened.
3. Broken - permanently opened.

Your windows can be decorated in many different ways:

Fabric Drapes - These provide light control, regulate air flow and provide privacy before they get eaten by the vacuum cleaner. They are available in traditional or contemporary stylings and are easily affordable if you happen to be the Duchess of Windsor.

Curtains - Curtains are more informal than drapes and generally hang closer to the window before blowing out the window you inadvertently left open during the monsoon.

Fabric Shades - Went out with spats.

The Sunday Funnies -America's most popular window treatment, they add color and warmth to a room while providing privacy and are surprisingly affordable.

Hard Treatments - Blinds, pleated shades, shutters and boards nailed to the outside of the house. These are slightly colder window treatments but they do have the distinct advantage of providing a home for every wayward speck of dust in the neighborhood.

Part Eight

Accessories
to Murder

Accessories are the lifeblood of the home. They are what separates your home from everyone elses. Accessories can house important memories, they can serve as background to a room or as the room's focal point.

Your accessories fall into these basic categories:
Useful - China, table settings, jars, clocks, and pillows.
Pointless - purely decorative items such as crafts and photos.
Chipped - What most of your accessories are.
Your Children's Toys - These are scattered about the room in a random manner adding new excitement and adventure to walking.
Crumbs - You tell them not to eat in there but they still do.
Loose Change - An attractive addition to any piece of upholstery.

Part Nine

Get a Grip

Relax, this is not as serious as you think it is.

This is not life and death. It's Interior Design.

Don't take yourself or your interiors so seriously that you freak out if a coaster or magazine is out of place.

Your house is your home, not a museum. Live in your rooms.

Into Action!

You've got it all now. Courage, Confidence, Knowledge and Skill.

Your life and lives of your loved ones will improve dramatically by applying the principles put forth in the preceding chapters.

Your efforts will reward you with many years of comfort and happiness. You will experience feelings of self-satisfaction and serenity while increasing your enjoyment of living itself. You are ready! Ready to design like the pros! And, remember kids...

Don't Try This At Home!

English To Decoratorese
A Glossary of Useful Design Terms

Acanthus: A stylized leaf used as a decorative motif resembling, when used in groups, that place in your backyard near the garbage cans that the tractor mower can't get at.

Antique: **1.** Furniture or other works of art that must be over 100 years old. **2.** The junk of a previous generation.

Apron: 1. Flat plane placed at a right angle below a shelf or top. **2.** What you wear when you cook.

Baroque: 1. Italian 16th Century art form utilized throughout Europe. Large, grandiose and overly curvilinear, the style was used primarily to impress guests. **2.** Popular 50's game show, *Go For Barouque.*

Bullnose: 1. Flat surface rounded at the edge. **2.** A bull's nose.

Buffet: 1. Dining room piece used for storage or serving.
2. Jimmy.

Charger: 1. A large serving dish. **2.** A Plymouth.

Check: 1. Cracks in wood. **2.** What you'll be signing alot of to get this stuff.

Chroma: 1. The relative intensity of a color.
2. What's on the bumper of your car.

Classical: 1. Referring to decorative motifs of Roman or Greek origin. **2.** A form of Coca-Cola.

Drier: 1. Chemical agent which causes paint to dry.
2. What you put your clothes in.

Eclectic: 1. Combining art forms. **2.** A mess.

Finial: An ornament incorporated at the top of a piece such as a lamp. **2.** Character in Joyce's famous work, *Finial's Wake*.

Fret: 1. Grecian motif used as a border. **2.** What you do when your children play in your living room.

Intaglio: 1. Indented decoration. **2.** Great with red wine.

LAF: 1. Left Arm Facing. **2.** To find amusing.

Marlborough Leg: Straight leg with a block-like foot.

Marlboro Man: Rugged individualist intent on dying from cancer.

Oriel Window: 1. Projecting window of Tudor English use. **2.** Stained glass featuring Brooks Robinson.

Parquet: 1. Wooden floor patterned by using strips. **2.** Butter!

Pompeii: Small, unimportant resort town erupted all over by Mt. Vesuvius in 76 A.D. thereby preserving the town in original state much to the delight of archeologists and the dismay of its ancient inhabitants.

Railroaded: 1. Fabric pattern applied up the bolt or running vertically. **2.** What happens when you buy from a slick sales person.

Right-Way 1: Application of fabric to a piece of upholstery in a particular fashion with pattern running from left to right. **2.** Not your way.

Splat: 1. The central strip of wood used in chair backs. **2.** The sound that occurs when paint hits the floor.

Stretcher: 1. Horizontal support used to connect furniture legs. **2.** What you'll be carried out on once you see the bill.

Tracery: 1. Stone mullions in Medieval windows. **2.** Cartoon character with two-way wrist radio, Dick.

Tudor Arch: Pointed arch used in English gothic buildings, precursor to Four-Door Arch.

Upholstery: 1. Cushioned seating furniture. **2.** Opposite of downholstery.

Veneer: Sheets of wood thinly cut and applied to a central core.

Weft: 1. Threads running crosswise. **2.** The opposite of Wight.

Welt: 1. Cording used on upholstery to hide seams. **2.** What will appear on your shin after you bump into the coffee table.

OTHER TITLES BY GREAT QUOTATIONS PUBLISHING COMPANY

199 Useful Things to Do With A Politician
201 Best Things Ever Said
A Lifetime of Love
A Light Heart Lives Long
A Teacher Is Better Than Two Books
As a Cat Thinketh
Cheatnotes On Life
Chicken Soup
Dear Mr. President
Don't Deliberate...Litigate
Father Knows Best
For Mother - A Bouquet of Sentiment
Golden Years, Golden Words
Happiness Walks On Busy Feet
Heal The World
Hooked on Golf
Hollywords
I'm Not Over The Hill
In Celebration of Women

Interior Design For Idiots
Life's Simple Pleasures
Money For Nothing,Tips For Free
Motivation Magic
Mrs. Webster's Guide To Business
Mrs. Webster's Dictionary
Parenting 101
Reflections
Romantic Rendezvous
The Sports Page
So Many Ways To Say Thank You
The ABC's of Parenting
The Best Of Friends
The Birthday Astrologer
The Little Book of Spiritual Wisdom
The Secret Language of Men
Things You'll Learn, If You Live Long Enough
Women On Men

GREAT QUOTATIONS PUBLISHING CO.

1967 Quincy Court
Glendale Heights, IL 60139-2045
Phone (708) 582-2800
FAX (708) 582-2813